T0303699

All the Bayou Stories End with Drowned

All the Bayou Stories End with Drowned

poems

Erica Wright

Black Lawrence Press

www.blacklawrence.com

Executive Editor: Diane Goettel
Book and Cover Design: Amy Freels

ISBN: 978-1-62557-971-3

Published 2017 by Black Lawrence Press.
Printed in the United States.

Contents

I

II

III

I

Lola and the Apocalypse

She sees catastrophe in every crow,
in every knocked-down clothesline—mostly

volcanoes and floods but sometimes scourges,
blue tongues, waves that forget their place

and storm into cities. Her mind stops at flesh peeling
back from the bone until it's white as milk,

the kind that makes grown men grow breasts,
and they feel that this is a catastrophe, but it's not.

Once when men were automobiles, the roads were slick
with sweat. They gleamed. Days were lost

to spectatorship, making bets on which color would rise up
out of the dark. Our girl made twenty dollars

on violet, but someone stole it. Who knows who?
It was hard to tell one chrome from another.

You couldn't cross for fear of getting hit, a parade
of reds and browns. And maybe the afterlife is a bookshop,

and she's been good, so she'll get to loiter
by Pop Culture/Crime instead of Business/Money.

From her perch, she'll count personality types. The schizotypals
will never object when she fondles their frontal lobes,

that gray, dirty satin. Elbow-deep in it. Her epigraph will remain
unwritten because there's no one left to scrawl platitudes:

For every pain, there is a duck with your name on it.
    But there aren't any ducks. At ponds worldwide, they ate

each other when no guests tossed crumbs and shooed away
    the geese that strike as if their bodies are lit fuses.

When cities were coal mines, the children played
    color games, too, but it was hard to determine a winner.

Lola knew a man there who didn't balk at anything, could stare down
    whatever slime-bellied beast approached their home.

She can't recall his name, but it could have been Roger.
    They had books, too, mostly Cultural Studies.

"Maybe I'm not alone," she thinks. "Maybe the devil stalks me
    right this minute, wants me to run, make it more *exciting*."

Lola sits down on the nearest ledge. "Ha," she thinks. "Haha."
    She doesn't notice the fissure at first. It sneaks

between floorboards, and when she pries them apart,
    her fingertips bleed in protest. They drip

onto the bleach-white worms that catch fire in the light.
    And then the floor collapses and then the world.

The survivors are called hostages or will be
    if any are met. Hostages in pines, hostages in barns,

hostages in the great wide open
    that makes them feel slit, wrist to armpit, in littleness.

Insurance of the Future

Peeling fingers can mean nothing
but shingles, and human-sized amoebas

lurk in every tunnel, like the time a bear
of a man emerged in the dusk to ask

for directions, then change, then what
to do when galaxies collide and we rip

from the pressure, crotch to throat.
Are we a new species then? Or are we gone

the way of ancestral mammoths?
Quirks of survival leave us roaches

but not pterodactyls. So much for majesty.
So much for writing a letter to your best lover

and explaining his pulse on your back
makes up for rising in the dark, suiting up

to step out into the Milky Way, yes,
but also into a void you can't touch.

Slick with cayenne and stardust,
let's make an advertisement for despair:

> *Welcome to planetary warfare!*
> *Do you know much about lasers?*
> *Where do you see yourself in five hundred years?*

I see myself in a spacesuit riding a mammoth,
trying to diagnose myself from fever and scabs,

and according to the internet,
I may not even be human. It's that bad.

The Twin Nature of Wedding Guests

The groom gets drunk enough to lose
 the feeling in his hands and invents

a cure for loneliness by accident.
 Who needs inoculation?

The bystanders have never known such
 promise and take it out on each other.

There's a ride home with too much
 singing for those who still have the ache,

those who tuck their heads against the glass,
 watch their noses in reflection,

remember earlier trips in the backseat
 of Mom and Dad's Chrysler

when they thought their skin looked nice
 in the headlamps of other cars.

The driver wishes everyone
 could move faster along the highway,

longs for the quiet return,
 and this dual longing—

to be loved, to be left alone?
 There is no cure for it and never will be.

Spontaneous Human Combustion

You can't mask the scent of sulfur
once it sets in the upholstery.

That's as far as we've come in understanding.
Someone was here, and now he's not.

Sometimes your insides want to become
your outsides, and you have to tell them "No."

I remember *chaud,* but have forgotten
the French for cold, the sensation

of needing to burrow, of nosing dirt aside
to bury myself in the basement's crawlspace.

There's a sound like swing-set chains
unwinding. Not like the time I snipped

my ring finger while maneuvering scissors.
Blood pooled, and there was no way

to test for tetanus. The great chasm of years
since inoculation weighed on me. Lockjaw:

as if a key went missing along with the ability
to tell someone, "Look out!

The sky hasn't looked friendly for days."
I do not like to argue, even with people I love,

but there's only accident out there in the flatlands,
bright as any phenomena, cruel as any store-bought pyre.

Disguised Weapons, Everyday Objects

With the right combination
        of numbers, a phone discharges

.22 caliber rounds, and that's enough
        to silence the witnesses.

Bedposts fall under
        "less spy, more convenient"

and can be wiped clean.
        All the women line their eyes

with kohl, let the points extend,
        and this is only dangerous in cases

of mistaken identity, doppelgangers.
        If you meet yours, kill yours,

even if your hands resist,
        refuse to break the windpipe

of yourself, but it's not yourself,
        only a mirror-image

with a better job, boyfriend,
        Labrador Retriever to your mutt.

We hunt a wild boar with spears
        made from brooms and cut mason jars.

If the boar spoke, he would tell the story
        of three little girls who used a pinafore

as leash and noose.
Marigold left school one afternoon

and came back a suitcase,
complete with destination stickers

for Barcelona, New Guinea,
and the Arctic Circle.

It's tricky to gauge the recoil
without television shows

that pit Apaches
against Maori Warriors

as if this weren't as awful
as little moon-faced killers,

you and me if we could disappear
as easily as we mind the gap, afraid

to have our bodies severed
by oncoming trains.

Truth or Dare

Ruby complained of blood blisters
and extra work shifts for snowing the cafeteria.

I wasn't there, but I had to scrub pots anyway.
This is how adolescence goes sometimes

unless you're a brat, and you're no goose,
my darling, you're no last-picked nor nicknamed.

I claim I lost my only bracelet on a dare,
messing around with another camper's letters,

as if anyone ever asked me to play games
of those sorts, ones with bottles the color

of outfields, the color of elsewhere.
Midnights were beyond me, filled as they were

with cardigans and the howling of some stuck beast,
lions in another lifetime, but there a coyote at best.

This was meant to be a love song, I can tell you now
that I've failed. It was meant to propose we build

a house, hang the rafters and the screen doors,
so no bats nor opossums could take us by surprise.

Once when I was camper-aged, I surprised
a rat snake nesting among keys and cassette tapes.

"Look," he said, "you don't need this corner of forgotten like I do."
So I let him be until those in charge

took charge with rakes and beheadings.
You don't want to marry me. I lose things.

Abandoned Doll Factory

The heads forever piked,
stripped of torsos, limbs, dresses
meant to imply animation—

that and the eye springs.
Lids sink and sleep
the sleep of toys and machines

left praying in the dawn.
Who's called by their insistence?
Out there beyond plywood

and bolts, do wayward teens mind
the warning signs or giggle
toward another bloated horror like

The Case of the Drowned Cosmetologist
or *Reports on Acid Baths & Gender Relations.*

They never ask about manifestos
scrawled on breakroom mirrors
the day the conveyors stopped.

They'd never see the mastermind
there anyway, taking paint
to the scooped-out cheeks.

Nobody's intended, these girls,
not the ones peering in
nor the ones peering out.

Age of Discovery

Space feels like scales moving under bare feet,
but we never trust the neighborhood astronaut.

He can say whatever he wants and still gloss up
the grocery magazine covers. Once, Sammy promised

protein shots, quick jolts in our shoulders,
but we're placebo-savvy, kids of cartoon dynamite,

how it never blows as directed, and anyway,
villains barter better than heroes, can lose

because they've lost before and survived the fallout.
Take pirates and their workman's comp: $800

for a limb lost while hailing kraken, then rueing
their own bravado when face-to-tentacle

with hand-to-god mayhem. A million miles up or down—
it's all the same trick in the handheld mirror,

the same twins mugging in the dressing room.
And Sammy, if you're still there, we confess

to bottle rockets in your driveway. We wanted to see
if they could travel past the radio tower beacon.

We thought whatever monster blinked up there
might want to know that was someone was trying—

however many light years away from success—
trying with the far-flung hope of future explorers,

our backpacks heavy with unread guidebooks,
knowing the difference between you can and you must.

Inventory at Thirty-Three

We got invites to Tampa burning
through our pockets, and when we arrive,

we'll swap swamp lies for gasoline
to keep this car running. We got jumper cables

snaking around a spare in the trunk
and no use for expired license plates.

We bet on red every time like holy rollers
gripping hymnals until their palms bleed

onto their witness. We're saying
we got a roadmap but no roads that want us.

Down along the highway, we close our eyes
and will traffic into tides, every hint of tar

into a starfish rotting on something
called Beach Blanket Row.

Then there's that miner's cough
from whatever acids we gulped

in the footprints of the country's tallest buildings.
We got a racking that comes and goes.

In the kitchen, there's a school of dead fish
in the pipes. These are ours, too:

a handful of coins for the meter, an excuse
about holes in our uniforms

and only one of us ever learned how to sew
and even then, only buttons.

Still we rip the blue with our canines
and try again. When we were small,

it snowed onto our backs while we slept,
and we kept this ache inside us

for show and tell. The other kids yawned
their reviews, pulled gangrene and jaundice

from their backpacks, and we knew
we'd always meet our matches,

but then again we'd always find another
loose nail to throw with the others

so that, given a gift of lumber, we could
build ourselves a home right here

in this pavement weed tangle
no one's bothered with for years.

Oracle for the Violin's Daughter

In a basement cold enough
to store meat, you assemble boxes.

Your fingers go numb,
and you fumble each fold,

but still make origami
from cardboard, imagine giraffes

in the backyard, stretching themselves
into gutters to nuzzle at run-off.

You remind me of the girl
who gathered oysters

until the tide took her away.
You're that kind of deserter,

a master of moving, the envy
of every knocked-up teenager,

every hounded spouse.
Touring tabernacles a decade hence,

men will stare to the right
of your right ear as if heaven

resides over a stranger's shoulder.
They will speak of medicine

and its limits, how a child could
survive amputation and soldering.

"What do prophets know and how?"
they'll ask. You will say nothing

then describe the alchemy,
how the story ends with pieces

of the body being tossed
from a convenient window.

Migration of a Minor God

You're no sun god gambling the moon god
for more days in the year, no siren asking

for more love from as-good-as-gone men.
Your chanting is the sound of cars hitting gravel

in the rain, and it won't stop pouring,
so you try higher notes. It's not cannibalism,

digging feathers from your side,
not even when your incisors scrape and snip.

Like gnawing splinters out of cuticles,
or better yet, letting someone else do it.

You preferred ticks, the painless tug
after touching their backs with blown-out matches.

Then the exit through the screen door,
the endless field of injuries.

"What must everyone think of me now," you ask.
Today you hide your molting under coats,

walk this town in a partial faint, no better than
run-of-the-mill angels using fog machines and flashlights.

The point is coming back anyway, a little more
spent, a little more dead than the same time last year.

Lola and the Wolfhound

For awhile there are two mouths at least,
 one human girl and a grizzled beast too shook

to do much more than rack his teeth together.
 The sound becomes a way to measure time,

each hour equals thirty clicks of his jaw.
 She records variations, not only the dog's

mange—the great patches of skin
 to tease themselves into view—

but also the shingle to arrive one morning
 without a house in sight. Once, the sky fills

with ash, and she chokes it down
 with all the other intrusions. *Click, click.*

When her lungs revolt, she coughs
 red globs into the air where they hang

like eyes and turn wherever she turns,
 so that if some day crowds arrive, they'll see

a whole jury ready for a witness.
 "Huh," thinks Lola, pulling the collar straight.

"Maybe they're on their way now,
 farm implements in tow. We should hear them out."

And she lets her sentries swivel in the night,
        bathe the floor of her canyon with drippings.

No one could accuse her of welcome-wagoning,
        of sucking up to governors

when there are none and haven't been
        for a million clicks, maybe more.

She hopes she won't feral out before the end,
        let her own whiskers gray until, lying down

muzzle to muzzle, there's no telling the two apart
        anymore. Where do her teeth end and his begin?

II

American Ghosts

These see-throughs want to shake your hand,
none of this calling out to mirrors, letting

daughters burn their locks with matches.
Today they assemble. When sure that all

are present and outfitted with hymnals,
they vote, push the light from their palms

until bells ring like rivers cracking in spring.
These hollows, these nobodies with veto power

swear at cemetery gates, wipe the rust
with mourners' pocket squares.

Widows, widowers, and their single compatriots,
they remember the weight of boots,

prefer the company of dust,
wouldn't bother a sleeper for the world.

Their eyes are streams filled with trout
enough for villages, their stomachs thickets.

In ribcages nationwide, the beetles nest,
make songs only the dead can hear,

ditties about battles and crowd control.
If they approach with their mouths

full of gold, ask "Alaska or California?"
Then offer your first and last name,

middle initial if the one nearest counts
losses in years, and who wouldn't?

Outside the perimeter, the newly gone
get lectures on haunting, choose

with a stupor that lasts until the blue hour,
declare that they don't need this land anymore.

Nimbus

Heaven hovers six feet above the parquet,
and you can run your fingers through it
and still not believe. This is how faith strikes

some of us: a man-made cloud disappears
as soon as it can. No caged beast, it scurries,
reports back to the others that there's nothing

worth seeing down there in what are called cities.
I'm considering how small my own city has grown
as I wait in line for a unisex bathroom,
nodding along as a fellow patron preaches.

His sermon's called,
"In Defense of Plasticity and the Deviance of Mankind"

and features breasts and soda bottles.
He's not talking to me. I make it inside the stall,
but can still hear him, and I want to flush myself away

from a world in which even sun-kissed skin is artificial,
and yet there's that cloud, and it makes my eyes swell
in awe the way landlocked recruits must feel

seeing the ocean for the first time, then not believing
the stories of how luminescent fish are really lost sailors
blinking to the surface, returning to say
that there's nothing worth seeing down there either.

Carpentry

First crawl underneath, suck in your gut and squeeze
past the central air duct. From your belly, you won't

see much, but you may get a sense of proportion
or a glimpse of something silver—opossum

or meat hook. Later when you lay hands
to the hardwood, do not be surprised if you unearth

something meaner, if there is anything meaner left.
Once you leave your mother's house,

she will make short work of her own behemoth
with its three-razored mouths and entrails inside-out.

If you do not have a mother, do not start this project.
Shake out your sewing bag instead. Build a city.

Mortuary Man

Corpse-dust spills all over the floor,
and twenty brooms and bins

cannot erase the gray that settles.
The twenty alligators in the bathroom

eating from my hands do nothing
but nothing. Those scaly bastards

with their teeth spilling all over the floor—
beads for necklaces, if anyone cared

for the undertaker. Mr. Guts Face,
boys sneer on their way to baseball

and sheds stocked with 1970s porn,
full bushes like they will never see

in their lifetimes, though they will dream
of single brown curls on the sheets.

Their wives will crow about this and that,
but at least they have wives in this future.

At least there are more
than hours, oak, stain, and bleach.

Hollow

Never the water so much
            as the persistence, how even
a trickle, even a drop can cause
            the forehead to blister, then burst,
leaving only what's raw.
            This wound never gangrenes—
always washed, always clean—
            but we must walk around
with the gape, must speak
            to the bank teller and later the grocer
or at least the girl who bags
            our oranges. She isn't yet troubled
by Bactin or meteorology.
            Today the girl, Clara or Cassie,
will save five dollars
            and eight cents in a Band-Aid tin
she keeps in her toilet tank.
            If we follow her home
to Bayside where the bridges revolt
            with their mortar and expanses,
Clara will cut us,
            but not where we want,
and on the ride home, the relief
            will only swell the coming sting.

River X

In the nearby town of S—, the unfinished bridge
    waits for signage. Cars wait on either side for years,

neat rows of impatience, while the roadside diner
    courts new arrivals: *1937 Special: 30-Cent Burgers.*

Inside, Hazel has grayed then dyed then given up.
    They should call it after me, she thinks and thinks

she sees whales on the highway beginning
    to shake their marbled flukes toward the other shore.

The tribe tries to name the river each year,
    and once the youngest son of the barber drowned.

For days, the papers ran with "The Warning River"
    until Kaliska, "Coyote Chasing Deer,"

sent a letter on offensiveness and its causes.
    The list contained many wrong names.

The Museum-Store Scam

There's nothing to buy here
          we don't already own:
plastic reliquaries
          from medieval gardens.
Let's postcard us instead.
          You won't be saying anything
about my escapades
          with machinery;
I won't be dusting dandruff
          from your jacket.
In August, the unicorn is stabbed,
          and also in September.
Every day, in fact,
          the lance is in the belly,
and without flood or fire,
          will stay. This is one reason
people pray for the end:
          to be dislodged.

American New Year

The stars kiss without moving
their mouths much. Their hands
stop the cold with animal skin.
You've got me cornered again,
too fool to have noticed the exit.
We drink our praise with strychnine,
or anyway, we mean to. Plastic flutes
will never be crystal, sure, will never
slit our tongues. On this list of goals,
"hiding" in ink that shows in black light
like crime scene splatter:

> *There are the brains, there are the hearts,*
> *there are the chewed up, unidentified parts.*

We swear we will never be as nice again
(and are right) but are wrong that it matters.

Select. Start.

It's hard to love men who played video games
as boys. It's hard when you can't picture them

skinning their knees on gravel or later sneaking
cigarettes behind school, filling their lungs with bitter,

then exhaling such lack of self-awareness.
They know the sunburned faces of life

when they see them. But these others who sank
into the flickering screens—thumbs swollen

over ladders, mushrooms, hedgehogs—
what can I know of them? When they ask me

to bed, I can't picture their faces turned
to the window as they reach over my bare everything

to turn the radio dial, and it's hard to say yes
to what you can't imagine. Think of your enemy

left alone, picking at scabs. Don't you want to take him
home now, the full-grown version whose hands

never know surrender? Don't you want them
to surrender to your diary, your treehouse,

your first rough time when you shuddered then tried
to forget your shuddering in the hum of our electronic days?

Admitted: There Are Tractors in This Hallucination

You breathe through a ratty mask
that makes you look like a surgeon
in some cesspool county—
one who'd rather kill than resurrect.
You've got your sights on a buck,

and I don't blame you. I don't look
like much under these fluorescents.
I don't look like I'm worth the effort
even though it says my name
right there on the insurance card.

I was once called a medical mystery,
but I wanted to be a marvel
with a colon big as a tuna, an eye livid
as piss. There are stones inside me
playing a child's game, and though it hurts

to flick my nail on marble, I need
to have the milkiest orbs. I need to win.
There's enough laudanum for one more
good run, and I'm bounding along
the highway where tractors idle

or get stuck. We'll pass them
on the shoulder 'cause there's room
enough for both of us on this endless stretch
of road where up ahead embers glow
before they're caught and fed to the machines.

Discrepancies

My face rearranges, and it's beginning
    to trouble me. The new passports, glasses,

fear of the bedroom mirror,
    that there's someone else here besides me.

Will this forehead bring you back?
    Should I disguise my voice, *sotto voce*,

charm you with the lies I know you'll like?
    My breasts may give me away,

but my hips are lower somehow.
    The truth is, we can be addicted to anything:

the hymns of witness next door or letting
    the RPMs rise dangerously before shifting.

I've grown taller—not taller—thinner and could crack
    in two given the right application of weight.

Each morning, an unveiling:
    let's see if the parts still work.

Bed Rest

The doll can sit up on its own,
if that's what you're asking.

It's not a real girl no matter
the umbilical cord, the mew

and soft thighs. All limbs
end in glass. Somewhere

a maker demanded feathers
in all the unexposed parts,

the hollow belly awaiting
its liver and heart. It's true

that when you dangle Baby
by her legs, her eyes close.

What of it? Mother responds
with ash on the crawlspace

where playthings could be
stowed, but never are.

Yesterday someone said
she looked ready

for the firing squad.
She's been told as much before,

could be her spine is no more
real than the stitches,

not a row of bones, but a rupture,
sewn-shut but still visible,

I'm guessing. What is it
that makes flesh ready

for a bullet? Its speed?
Its do-or-die whistle?

She's got her shoes on.
She's got some time left.

Nashville

The city bachelor parades for magazines,
preens in elevator doors to whistles in his head,

and in this way swallows the jitters hot-stepping
in his gut. Where are the love-starved layabouts

rooting for his fame? He wonders,
where are the noisemakers and the manicured

villains who boil their bloody clothes in the dawn?
This is not the music of futures

his mother had hoped for, lobbied for
in a mix of Father and coke-laced rootwork.

But slide guitars sound sweet-licked and confessed.
Sing the verse nobody likes to hear while driving,

the one about ladies mainlining relief
in not choosing one doe-eared lad over another.

Sing in that timbre nobody hears without wanting
to kick up dust bridges guarding dust rivers.

Years ago they swept debris into nowhere anyone looked.
Now sing in lime-caked hollows, son, or do not sing at all.

Paralysis and Football Américain

When I say I'm not agoraphobic,
I don't deny mornings curled

on the floor, refusing to uncoil
so the outer reaches of my limbs

won't get taken. I confess there is
evidence, but at the same time,

across the country, boys suit up
in plastic meant to keep them

from harm while they hurl
themselves into harm, repeatedly.

Death, I will chase you in stadiums.
I will be ready when you turn

on me with your rows of eyes.
For once, my arms will swing

when I tell them to, and at their ends
will be all manner of weapon.

Art in the Age of Popularity

We counted, and this is our one clue:
parades without chant or whistle,

a muted tumble of mourners or winners,
it's been too silent to tell for days.

But oh how polite in our handshakes,
our waving from across the street,

"hello!" as we take our trash to the bins,
"hello!" as we take no notice of the flies,

how their bodies are fat with the filth
we crave, but we do everything right.

We do nothing right. "Hello again!
You look like someone someone could love."

We look like sunscreen and Vitamin D
supplements, like burns wouldn't dare,

wouldn't scar up this place for the world,
and it's cleaner in the light where sidewalks

extend as far as we'll ever see,
wilderness at bay until further notice.

Our Wilderness Period

We caravanned from the city, then trickled
          until—looking around—it was solo hiking,

each with her backpack full of canned goods.
          The gravel clicked and slid, but there was nowhere

on that state park highway but more forest.
          What I'm saying is I don't like being alone

like this, praying that the treeline doesn't swing into battle.
          Even if the others were here, they couldn't stop

the limbs from pulling back their weapons,
          letting loose fire-tipped arrows to smoke us out.

I recall the monsters of my youth, the mirror faces
          waiting for mistakes, one name said three times,

but I taped my mouth shut, too clever by half
          for the girls' bathroom. There's a name for shouting

at funerals or imagining you will until your only hope
          is digging the hymnal into your thigh,

Christian soldiers hiding their bayonets
          but not in time to stop the scarring.

In the clearing, someone stacked rocks
          into steeples. I can kick those down, too,

forget we ever dined together at cafes,
the waiters impressed by our jokes.

Weren't we the hours then? Weren't we
the soapbox heroes, silencing our phones

and pointing out the exits?
We knew how to act at the movies,

even when the actors broke down,
forgot if their lovers were Angelas or Bessies,

pushed the boom mics with handkerchiefs
embroidered for screen-time crying jags.

In the red emergency light, we were vixen-ready, too,
careening into a night crisp with bit players.

Now I sleep in half-hour cycles, watch the perimeter.
We could take turns if here together,

split firewood duties, whittle our own axes, then squint
at the constellations hard until Andromeda

thinks we're winking, ready enough for the fold.
But the point must be the quiet, the prep work

for end credits, and when we're finally ready
to monologue, we get to assemble again,

let out the keen that doesn't mean as much
since we don't mourn our friends when we're with them.

American Highways in Billboard Country

The ads lie breathlessly,
silk their way into our cars

until we wonder if models
comb their hair with olive oil

or if the shine comes from a diet
of Pepsi and trail mix,

$3.99 at the Winn-Dixie
across from the laundromat.

This is no town we'll stop in,
but what if the mayor plans

in his sleepless nights a jubilee
even better than the last one,

so good that teens will show off
their braces in delight, fawn over

the truckload of athletes
and the gleam of another tuba.

What if the exit we choose
isn't the one we wanted?

Each slate sings of late-night fever,
how headlights make us ache

for passengers in other cars,
their paper bags of takeout

scenting the upholstery. Up ahead,
a tractor trailer hits the shoulder,

rights itself like a whale smacking
back into the gulf, its huge body

finding other huge bodies
somehow in the dark.

III

All the Bayou Stories End with Drowned

Even the fairytales resort
    to air machines as if we can't keep

our boys and girls above water for very long.
    "Some jaws got him. I seen 'em."

The blurry shoreline—
    here is safe, here is not—

or let's blame the treelight, it slithers
    and makes us call our neighbors,

but there really isn't anyone out there.
    The real haunting is the light itself.

Everything else ends with decision:
    skull crushed, heart stopped, bled.

Even aphids make patterns
    that can be imitated, cut into lace,

and the circles get smaller in the search
    as the townsfolk trawl into other landscapes.

Artificial Terrain

Why only a pond? Why not a forest
where visitors get lost, torn

between taking a right at the sycamore
or climbing up to see over the canopy?

You could make a quilt from the pieces
of ripped flannel. You could sew
with finger bones whittled to a point.

You'd never be cold or bored again
in your new kingdom. When twins disappear,
the pet grizzly could choose

between the ugly boy and the long-winded girl.
Then, why not kiss yourself in the mirror
where no one complains about a busted lip.

You want to be the one who swims,
not the one who says, "Hello, pond,
what've you got down here besides fish?"

I know what you're thinking:
What do I know of cartilage and slick?

Not much, not much.

But that down-below world is blue-balls mean,
and we run so hot that we pulse with it,
the not enough, the never enough, the keep going.

Hidden

Why do children find the dead ones?
Prod the vole, the bat, the lizard

with convenient sticks, turn carcasses
until the biggest organs are spotted.

This show and tell brings hoards,
a growing cohort of someday coroners.

Do their parents run? Like the time
your mother fetched a black snake

for your inspection, gripped its neck
but gentle as a cat carting all her kits

but the runt into the basement.
Beyond the yard, what skeletons

were hung up in classrooms?
What could these kids teach themselves?

You were safer in the brambles, you know.
At least from ministrations.

You can escape the poisons
if you wash them off your calves,

scrub with the faith of witches
stirring up their lye, buying bird beaks

from May who saves the best for herself.
She flees, too, sometimes, drops

into the drawn waters of a bathtub.
May resents the clean, but likes

when her armpits dangle over the sides.
You don't believe in such stews?

Here, let me show you this burrow,
let me have your hand.

State Bear

When the grizzly eyes you
then moves on grinning,

you've been tricked by a man
in a bear suit. Like when

you swear your blood coagulates
into patterns that mean something,

that you're an oracle or something
based on the edges of a drop—

this means war, this means a girl
will poison herself with cherry pits

but it will be an accident—
don't wander so far in a forest.

Once inside, even the birds grow
teeth in their mandibles.

They don't kid around.
Or if you must, you must,

but take me with you when you slide
into the bark and growl.

First Rabbit in the Clearing

A child jerked by his elbow straightens
what can be straightened: his story book,

his t-shirt and backpack. *This is not my mother,*
he gestures, but doesn't gesture, *no one outsmarts*

no one or perhaps, *ever, she is lost to me.*
If someone massages her eyebrow, she broods

not over bone structure. Not every time at least.
Sometimes after the parable ends, a fox suns

in a clearing, keeps his black eyes open.
He can stay all day, belly full of rabbit.

Zoology 101

With whole chapters torn from our textbooks,
we taught ourselves the way Slack-jawed
Mirror Bison crane their necks toward the light,

and we know what happened to the boy
who rode them into the blue mountains.

He's around here somewhere, ghosting
up the tourist cameras, telling his life story
of fire and formaldehyde. And we know

the Aggravated Tortoise can live
to be a million years old in turtle years.
Distended means a surgeon polishing
his own silver. Miniature means a child

refusing to speak for fear of mispronouncing
her own name. Our neighbor leaves the phone

off the hook while traveling, and all day
the beeps race like Sealhounds, hunting
a prey that never was, treeing a Fluorinated
Opossum. "Come over here, opossum,"

we say. "We know taxidermy. We know relief."

After the Human Pin Cushion: Mabel

She cuts the fingers of her mistress
          clean off and practices scales with them,
all those sharps and flats heavy
          with *rigor mortis.* Her paws never
carpal tunnel, and this is a neat trick:
          The Preeminent Four-Handed Pianist!
Each morning, she takes the digits
          from the formaldehyde, rubs them
with baby oil. But this is not
          what she meant, this fame, this bloodless.
Intent so rarely means love letters
          with fresh ears that listen to petulance,
or a forest where every bit of undergrowth
          bends to little girl feet, those pink, little boats.

Music for the Death-Defying

"Rosacea is all the rage, but not yet the pox,"
        says Mother Hen who Child Eliza once believed
truly feathered. Eliza runs toothless lions
        no longer. Everyone's seen that trick,
and the pets refuse their dentures,
        would rather flick their tails at parking lots.
"Marry, Eliza," but who and what for?
        She takes the knocks instead like the others.
"You'll one-day choke on your own fluff,"
        Mother Hen cursed at ten, but had no talent for it.
"You'll one-day wish," she'd start, then throw out
        "trampled" when she meant "skinned."

New World Explorers

With or without tailfin,
this plane goes nowhere
but circumnavigates the boy
who holds it as close
to somewhere as possible:
the window and also the poster
of Jorge Posada and the ceiling fan
if he leaps from the top bunk.
Downstairs, the table is set
with four yellow plates
though at least one's an extra.
Domesticity is for the birds,
thinks the boy's mother,
sucking on another
grease burn. This one
is shaped like Florida.
Another Ponce de Leon
look-alike bangs on her door.
She doesn't bother to peek out
the curtains this time.
They've all the same mustache
and lack of table manners.
"Dinner," she calls as her boy thuds
back down to the ground.
He makes motor noises
and misses the man altogether.

Festival Circuit

Crowned beauties smile with teeth
            strong enough to bite through necks

of prey or even the predators
            they sometimes grasp behind their heads,

nonchalant about the venom.
            Who has time for poison

when shotguns gleam twice as bright,
            sometimes fire of their own volition?

"People first," Carmen trills
            while keeping tabs on her neighbors,

their penchants for novelty mailboxes.
            She's a girl raised on raw beets

and paperback horror, so nobody trusts her
            alone with their pets. Yesterday, her motto

stumbled, stuck in the news cycle of pop star
            chemical weapons, and she hummed

theme songs, anything to keep her knees
            and feet facing the same direction.

It's not that far to Los Angeles.
            This town wants a hoodwink,

a hint of what little concrete keeps out.
Instead it gets hootenannies and fair booths

in praise of turnips, of grits,
of local creek water moonshine.

In praise of livestock, of machine operators,
their clavicles protruding like rusted-out gutters.

In praise of makeshift parking lots,
of grease, of Carmen saying, "*Buenos días,* y'all"

to the hooting of glamour-starved whistlers,
lust making the pigs nervous in their pens.

Trespassing

I thought I was done telling
about the copperhead, the arrow
of its head that points as if to say,

"I choose you despite your anemic eyes
and attic sleeping place, chilled
when the snow comes as it comes
every dark-lidded January.
You are no kind of heroine
because you watch the burned girl
in class without ever speaking to her."

Every part of that snake gleams
kettle-colored, hear the hiss
that says, "I'm ready for you."

And you deserve the punctures,
the sweet choke, the too far for help

because you shouldn't have been there
in that field, too big to ever belong
to a rag of a thing like you.

Alibi

We were nowhere near that farm, my wolf and me,
    except he's just the cowlicked neighbor's mutt.

The neighbor's name escapes me. The dog's Samson.
    I know because I hear the muffled cries:

"Samson, don't mind the storms."
    "Samson," it's me whispering this time,

"never mind the mess I've made."
    Beasts don't learn to live alone.

They're born into the forest, into roots and into maggots.
    This is its own luxury, never missing

what was never yours. Never mind, Samson.
    I can see you from here,

pulling at your tether until the rope meets skin,
    rubs raw the same place as yesterday.

Accomplice

When lined up by guilt,
            the first boy slipped
his knife to another
            who must have known,
and this was the beginning
            of conspiracy. All of us waited
for the reeds of retribution:
            "Pick out your own switch."
Every con, every fallen branch,
            was weighed until we came up
empty and aching for redemption.
            We thirsted at the entryway
where we were met by the chlorine
            scent of modern baptism.

American Burial Rites

God says we get the timbre
            wrong, let rain fall too fast
onto our wool and leather.
            We only ever try once,
blame mechanical failure
            and aunts who hide their gin
better than others. We love
            our dead, no question,
but cover the satin quick,
            slap the lids as if popping
pickups on their way.
            "Drive safe." Our sons
can't hear us over the engines,
            see our mouths flash teeth
then hide them. Mostly
            the time's about shovels
and how they're angled
            away from our unused bodies.
Ice deters us, but we break even
            earth to dispatch our offices.

Communion

We don't mention that kind of blindness
anymore. We don't drag our toolboxes

out in the middle of parking lots,
rearrange them according to color—

slate to red handle—then put them up again
because when everything's broken,

why start now? "Hush your mouth,"
says someone in the gas station.

There's church on Sunday,
and everyone has to look the preacher

in the eye to say goodbye, and everyone
has to say goodbye before they go home.

Maybe this is no town we've ever seen before,
just one with the same boarded-up school

and stove under that hollowed oak
that needs cutting down.

Inside, copperheads nest with rat snakes,
each with his task, each with his length

of bark in the evening. Yes, this could be
a different oak, this could be a different day

when all of us decide to leave,
            and then the car won't start.

We close our eyes instead and see stretches of highway,
            brand-spanking new off the assembly line.

We see silos that are towers in the right light,
            and the right light is among us now.

The metal beckons travelers to sidle up
            to its expanse, rest a bit before big-city limits

gobble them right on up.
            When we shift our loneliness to another hip,

the skin left behind is imprinted,
            acute angles that pulse until the blood pushes

everything smooth. This is not like scarring,
            not like running as only children can run,

without looking to see what's ahead, trusting that no one
            would throw something toward an abandoned well

for knees to hit with such force that,
            for a moment, nothing hurts at all.

Notes

1) "Spontaneous Human Combustion" is dedicated to Kristen Linton.
2) "Lola and the Apocalypse" is dedicated to Ricardo Alberto Maldonado.
3) "Nimbus" responds to Berndnaut Smilde's indoor clouds, specifically "Nimbus II."
4) "Bed Rest" responds to Frida Kahlo's "Yo y mi muñeca."

Acknowledgments

Thank you to the editors of the following publications.

B O D Y: "Carpentry," "Discrepancies," and "Mortuary Man"
BOMB Magazine Word Choice: "Hollow"
Cavalier Literary Couture: "Accomplice"
Cimarron Review: "Truth or Dare" and "American Highways in Billboard Country"
Crazyhorse: "Lola and the Apocalypse"
DIALOGIST: "Festival Circuit"
Drunken Boat: "All the Bayou Stories End with Drowned"
Gulf Coast: "Disguised Weapons, Everyday Objects" and "Spontaneous Human Combustion"
Joe + Gigs: "Bed Rest"
The New Orleans Review: "State Bear" and "First Rabbit in the Clearing"
Notre Dame Review: "Artificial Terrain" and "Select. Start."
The Philadelphia Review of Books: "Oracle for the Violin's Daughter" and "The Twin Nature of Wedding Guests"
Ping-Pong: "Admitted: There are Tractors in This Hallucination," "Paralysis and Football Américain," "After the Human Pin Cushion: Mabel," "Music for the Death-Defying," and "New World Explorers"
Poetry Quarterly: "Hidden"
Slice Magazine: "River X"
Spinning Jenny: "Migration of a Minor God" and "Zoology 101"
TUBA: "Communion"
Vinyl: "Insurance of the Future" and "Trespassing"
White Whale Review: "The Museum-Store Scam"

I am extremely lucky to have such supportive friends and family. Thank you to Ricardo Maldonado and Matthew Pennock who were instrumental in making this book. It has been a dream to work with Black

Lawrence Press again, particularly Diane Goettel and Angela Leroux-Lindsey. I appreciate the encouragement of Kristen Linton, Katie Meadows, Tayt Harlin, Toral Doshi, Chris Shiflett, Adam Province, and so many others. Thanks to *Guernica Magazine* for ten years of inspiration. I end this too-little note of gratitude with love for my parents, Kevin and Paula Wright.

Photo: Paula Wright

Erica Wright is the author of the poetry collections *All the Bayou Stories End with Drowned* (Black Lawrence Press, 2017) and *Instructions for Killing the Jackal* (Black Lawrence Press, 2011). Her poems have appeared in *Crazyhorse, Denver Quarterly, Gulf Coast, New Orleans Review,* and elsewhere. She is the poetry editor at *Guernica Magazine* as well as an editorial board member of Alice James Books. Her latest novel is *The Granite Moth* (Pegasus, 2015).